The Bearable Slant of Light

The Bearable Slant of Light

poems

Lynnell Edwards

Red Hen Press | Pasadena, CA

Book design by Luis Ramos

Library of Congress Cataloging-in-Publication Data

Names: Edwards, Lynnell, author.
Title: The bearable slant of light: poems / Lynnell Edwards.
Description: First edition. | Pasadena, CA: Red Hen Press, 2023.
Identifiers: LCCN 2023040159 (print) | LCCN 2023040160 (ebook) | ISBN
    9781636281285 (paperback) | ISBN 9781636281292 (ebook)
Subjects: LCGFT: Poetry.
Classification: LCC PS3605.D8895 B43 2023 (print) | LCC PS3605.D8895
    (ebook) | DDC 811/.6—dc23/eng/20230908
LC record available at https://lccn.loc.gov/2023040159
LC ebook record available at https://lccn.loc.gov/2023040160

The National Endowment for the Arts, the Los Angeles County Arts Commission, the Ahmanson Foundation, the Dwight Stuart Youth Fund, the Max Factor Family Foundation, the Pasadena Tournament of Roses Foundation, the Pasadena Arts & Culture Commission and the City of Pasadena Cultural Affairs Division, the City of Los Angeles Department of Cultural Affairs, the Audrey & Sydney Irmas Charitable Foundation, the Meta & George Rosenberg Foundation, the Albert and Elaine Borchard Foundation, the Adams Family Foundation, Amazon Literary Partnership, the Sam Francis Foundation, and the Mara W. Breech Foundation partially support Red Hen Press.

First Edition
Published by Red Hen Press
www.redhen.org

Acknowledgments

Thanks to Red Hen Press for their belief in this manuscript and their careful shepherding of its publication.

Thanks to poet and dear friend Doug Van Gundy for his thoughtful reading of this work and his conversations about poetry, life, and all that feeds it. And to poet Lisa Krueger for her many insights and keen eye that helped make the manuscript more vital, abundant gratitude.

To Maggie Smith and Tom Sleigh, many thanks for their generous and brilliant endorsements of this work.

To Charlotte Pence for her careful reading and comments on several problem poems, to Martha Greenwald for her listening ear as these poems began taking shape, and to my colleagues at the Sena Jeter Naslund-Karen Mann Graduate School of Writing for their support of my writing, much appreciation. I am thankful to the Hermitage Artist Retreat for granting me the great gift of time and space to complete this manuscript.

Thanks to our family and many friends who have listened and consoled and helped carry the burden of our grief and lightened the load with their friendships.

And finally, to my partner and husband Wes, in this and all that follows, gratitude and love.

Acknowledgment is made to the following where these poems first appeared in print:

Action, Spectacle: "Medical history #2" and "Walgreens: everything plus your meds" (originally: "Walgreens: at the corner of happy and healthy"); *Kestrel*: "Pareidolia"; *Miracle Monocle*: "Blood sport sabbath," parts I and III; *Plume*: "Security: A Q & A"; *Sou'wester*: "It's just been a difficult week" (originally: "I Thought They'd Be Giving Out Ambien") and "Pray for Rain"; and *Waccamaw*: "We Were talking about our father's guns" (originally: "We were talking about guns").

I'm not going to tell you my whole goddam autobiography or anything.
I'll just tell you about this madman stuff that happened to me . . .
—Holden Caulfield

Contents

IV. Whose gemstone is rain

The Bearable Slant of Light

Medical history #2

Me: I think there's a lot of trauma he has to process
Dr. K: Did something happen?!

The hospital happened   the involuntary happened   the injectables happened   *they had to rip his shirt*   the doctors the nurses the residents the techs happened   the other patients   some of them pacing in the hall   and loud   the first attempt happened   the one-on-one happened   the eeg happened   the ambulance happened   *none of this is in any kind of order you understand*   the restraints and psychosis   the overdoses and noncompliance   the catatonia the mania happened   the loneliness the isolation happened   *so many many different meds*   the assessments and telehealth happened   more ambulances happened the courts happened   the ect happened   the second attempt happened   the social workers happened   the intensive outpatients and treatment teams and therapists happened seven years happened   *he won't get them back*

I. Define self

NOW:

        text about
                your best friend, self-sacrifice,
some girl—half-imagined
                          mermaid of dazzle and rot.
      Don't they know how
            it all fits together? You're at the center
        of something. You are AT the center
of something.
              Write it down write
      it down and send it out:
the celebrity scandal
      and set-up: she's dead she's dead
              and it didn't have to be.
        And the internet trailer, don't they
     know?

It's coming together now it's
        coming together: the terrorist
and TV man, their secret code.

                          ~

This morning a chain saw
             gutters against the limbs   this morning
of magnolias grown too
                                      thick to persist
                                                     they twist
and choke the root
                 system, must be
cleared and heaped onto
         the trash pile: dead branches
dragged from the lake,
             insect-infected tree trunks, junk
lumber, broken shelves, broken
         deck chairs, planks from
the rotted dock—
                     all brought
                             to scourging blaze until
             across the property hangs
a mute haze, burnt
                 green and the taste of ash, grit
         on the skin that smears
                     to black, a red smolder,
something still
         to abrade and to burn all night

~

So here you are, big fella: single bed
in a clean room. No
electronics, no laces.

                    This is niiiice.
Give Dad the finger then
turn in. Let us figure out
the rest. You're tired,
we know.

                    ∾

HISTORY OF PRESENT ILLNESS: The patient is a 20-year-old white male with a reported history of ███████████████ that was diagnosed at a facility in ████████ approximately one week ago. The patient, per chart, experienced several days with no sleep and increased anxiety and agitation. He had an episode that is described as being somewhat catatonic. His mother had arranged to take him to see his outpatient psychiatrist, ████████. The patient reportedly ran from his mother and ████████ and then was intercepted by police. The policeman then reportedly brought the patient to ████ ███████████ where the mother met them.

On examination, the patient presents as a very poor historian. He has possible thought-blocking with possible psychosis. Potentially responding to internal stimuli. He reports that he went off Luvox that was prescribed by ████████ in ████████. The patient essentially denies any sympathology at the time he is interviewed by this physician. He denies mood swings. Per previous assessment, had suicidal ideation without overt intent or plan: however, he was unable to contract for safety.

～

Have there been changes in self-care?

Define care   define self   define change   he sleeps some   awake
at night a lot   appetite fine   sometimes helps with din-
ner   his clothes are   he keeps his apartment   he's a twenty
year old guy   he shaves sometimes   sometimes works out
he was   is   an athlete   he   he hasn't cut his nails in weeks

Have there been changes in patient's sleep patterns?

He's awake   a lot   I don't know how much   this last week   a
lot   I see the lights   in his room at night   he sleeps with all
the lights on   I found him   middle of the night   all the lights
on   arranging his bookshelves   I find him   middle of the day
asleep in his room   dark   he tells me: *mom   I don't have a
sleep cycle   look   see* he's fallen asleep there now   waiting

Does patient have access to a gun?

knives axe in the garage hedge clippers pruning shears ice pick
lawn mower blades scissors; rope wire twin bed sheets belts exten-
sion cords garden hose; antifreeze drain cleaner fertilizer gasoline
matches; bottles of whiskey bottles of pills what else   two cars
parked in the driveway to drive into a wall off an overpass into the
cloudy currents of the ohio river but no   no access to a gun

MENTAL STATUS EXAM: The patient was found laying in his bed. He is awake. He is alert and oriented x2. He is wearing hospital scrubs. He displays fair grooming and hygiene and is in no acute distress. He has normal gait. His musculoskeletal examination is within normal limits. His speech is soft but very delayed. His mood is described as being "fine." However, his affect is very flat with a very constricted range. Thought content without overt suicidal ideation or homicidal ideation, or auditory visual hallucinations reported. However, he appears to have thought-blocking and being responsive to internal stimuli. Thought processes, again, are very slowed and somewhat disorganized. Judgment and insight is essentially nil. Memory is poor.

∽

It is loud here, Dr. S. I cannot focus. The loud
TV and the loud woman who asks when
her daughter is coming, all the chatter,
the loud arts and crafts table, circle time
like I did in kindergarten, the creepy yoga—
Dr. S., it is so loud. I can do this
long enough (a day or three) to pass
for med-compliant before the live wires
of my thought tangle, my mind a runaway
truck on a mountain road, sparks,
the terrifying grind of brakes
on gravel. I am alone Dr. S., and it is dark.
 I have found the smallest safe place in my soul
and crouched there, an animal nosing out
in winter for food, the bearable slant of light in late day.

DISCHARGE TRANSFER SUMMARY: The Continuing Care Plan has been reviewed and discussed with the pt. He/she has been given an opportunity to ask questions. Within his/her current capabilities, the pt has considered the plan and: AWARE OF PLAN CONTENT.

Successful Comp: 1) Reg., consistent attendance, 2) comp. of 75% indv. treatment goals as written 3) transition to a lower level of care following dis.

Psychiatrist: Although, we provided these meds to you while you were hospitalized, you will NOT be given a prescription for them by your OLOP Psychiatrist. Instead, you will need to follow up with your prescribing provider ongoing care and refills.

The following medications were prescribed to you PRIOR to admission. They have been discontinued by your physician during your stay. DO NOT TAKE THESE MEDICATIONS!

Do you approve and agree to health information (includes Psychiatric Assessment, Discharge Summary, Psychosocial Assessment, History and Physical Examination, and the Continuing Care Plan) being sent to continuing care providers and your primary care physician on discharge?   Y

The patient/guardian was given the Record of Patient Rights?   N
Signature/Title: ███████████████████—LCSW

did you take your medication   I

took it   did you take

the morning ones the celexa the

ativan   I took it did you take it

the prn after lunch the ativan   I

took the meds I took them

all   did you take

the vistaril the serequol the risperdal

the geodon   I didnt take the geodon I dont

like the geodon I dont want that

one   what about the zyprexa did you take

the zyprexa yet   I took it   are you sure

I counted the zyprexa and theres still

9 zyprexa and there should be only

7 did you forget

maybe   did you take it last night   I dont

know I think so   what about the zyprexa

the night before I dont know   maybe

not I took the ativan

I know   but the zyprexa   the zyprexa is the one

that you cant miss you cant miss a dose or

will you take the zyprexa

now please take it now please

II. Its hiss and crackle

Reading a biography of Robert Lowell I think

You shan't be sorry, I will bring the steel and fire . . .
—Robert Lowell

enough already with the Puritan guilt,
New England winters, distant mother,
limpid father, deranged great-aunt
and the whole family treehouse,
skeletons rattling with frail nerves
and vacant days.   Enough
with the burden of privilege,
family crest on the Harvard dorm.
Enough with the precocity of childhood,
the signs are clear: oppositional,
compulsive, obsessive about all things
Napoleon, the collection of snakes
writhing out of drawers and closets
all summer. It's just a matter
of time. First one head doc,
then the next, pages of notes,
recommendations. Let's get
on to the train wreck, the pileup,
the full-blown break when he ascends
out of whatever sleepless, pacing,
rage he swims in, and descends,
hard landing in slippers, robe, old brick
and high windows, meals on a tray.
I read harder, faster though I know
Already how this will end. Outside
the cicadas are roaring. They're early
this year. Not even June and
already the whole world on fire.

What we observe is what we want to see:
axes elevated on Multiphasic Inventory II
for depression, anxiety, and here also see

severe, single episode, non-bizarre we see.
Cognitively normal across the board, too,
but ruminative without insight, unable to see

how the Thematic Apperception suggests he sees
dark horizons, dark valleys he is unable to
climb. And the evil surrounding he thinks he sees?

Combined with paranoia, though slight we see,
align with the Beck Depression, version two.
And the sleeplessness congruent, don't you see?

The delusions and mania, belief people see
his black soul, the pacing, and psychosis too
confirm the metrics and the history that we see.

Yes that's it exactly. Sort of. Here, you see:
your son, your boy, your man someday too
(but you have another one, don't you—two?),
we've charted him here, signed for you to see.

Dear F. Scott

Sometimes I didn't know whether Zelda
isn't a character that I created myself.
—F. Scott Fitzgerald

The letters, the landscapes, the records
from the clinics—where do we begin?
With innocence and gin? A soldier-boy
and a Montgomery girl? Dance cards fill
and the magnolias swoon and one girl
is made into another. They all drive
too fast, end in a smash-up. A party
gone wrong and late. Apologies and insolence.
Heaps of flowers filling the rooms. Which
girl stares across the water? Which girl
swims in the sea? Which one danced
to exhaustion and which one
scribbled stories? All the night streets
shine with rain. All the gas lamps halo
at dusk. The sun over the villa simmers
at noon and she picks at her lunch
of melon, champagne. All were beautiful,
white skin tanned to copper. Which girl
was mad, and which did you make so?
Rest cures and relapses; painting
en plein air. The doctor is a friend
or, are you the doctor? An old insult
is exorcised and she's free, moves on
with another man and leaves you. Or,
this: she fractures again and again,
spends long months with her mother,

people thought her strange. She
has to be sent somewhere.
You missed the ending so we'll tell
you here: there were bars
on the windows. That kind of place.
The outings were fewer and people
thought her strange. She painted,
marveled at the sun on the mountains.
Maybe things were getting better.
Maybe she would go home for good.
But there was a fire and the doors
were all locked. The wooden escapes
all burned and she was on the top
floor. The funeral was lightly
attended. Early March flowers
bloomed, bright in the warm air.

March mornings, three times a week, the city still dark and empty at 5 a.m., we drive to the hospital on empty streets. The garage park shines like day. We pull in, buzz for a ticket then park in short-term outpatient, second-story. You wear a stocking cap, dark canvas jacket, and sweats most mornings; I grip a cup of coffee getting cold and the newspaper still folded. There's no more uncertainty about where to go or what to do. We hurry through the automatic doors hissing their welcome.

Gold standard, preferred treatment, painless and safe; not like in the old days.

This is your second course of electroconvulsive therapy. We don't know how many sessions it will take or what will happen this time. The first course was at a hospital in St. Paul, Minnesota, where you were taken after a second psychotic break had panicked the college roommates you were living with while you worked on campus that summer. They called the crisis team after they watched you sit unmoving on the couch for three hours. This is what the dean told us. The report would say you had been acting strange for weeks before, that you thought people were changing your streaming station; that people were out to get you; that you started laughing uncontrollably then suddenly crying during weight training. You landed inpatient, for the third time, for two and a half months during which every diagnosis and failed medication finally led to the gold standard, preferred treatment, painless and safe; not like in the old days.

We were believers.   Educated and desperate. We read the success stories. We understood the science and the consequences (minimal) and results (maximal, though not sustained). *There is no definitive theory as to why ECT is effective for certain psychiatric conditions.* It causes a seizure in the brain. *It is not understood why a central nervous system seizure is effective treating depression and thought disorders.* You agreed. You had already missed preseason training and the start of the semester. There would be no return to school that fall.   After ten treatments the doctor pronounced it a success: fluidity of movement restored, the fog of depression lifted, thought-blocking and psychosis muted. You were discharged. You seemed whole, if not happy, when you came home, and we hoped this was a new path.

It was not.

Check-in: signature and bracelet, time-stamped parking receipt. Sometimes I sit with you in pre-op.   A nurse pulls the drape closed and I step out while you undress. There are warmed blankets and extra pillows. They ask how you're feeling while they connect the IV, take your vitals, confirm that you haven't eaten. I watch the medics busy with purpose: the whirr and flash of monitors. Carts stacked with sheets and towels and blankets rattle past: so much white fluorescence; everyone wearing pale blue. The floors shine. Sometimes I read to you from the news. I want to show you how okay this all is. Sometimes I do not stay to see you wheeled away.

How brave you were. How irrelevant and frail I felt.

We have seen the video: the patient sedated and mild on the bed. There are electrodes and wires, yes. There is a voltage meter and an anesthesiologist and an oxygen mask. There is a mouthpiece, yes.   It is not precisely a surgical setting; the attending medical staff wear white coats and stand near, ready to . . . help? There are no domed lights, no masked huddle busy and peering into a draped mound. There is a switch flipped and a buzzing hum as expected, but the only evidence of current is a slight trembling in the toe, a strange straight-armed lifting of the hands like, yes, Frankenstein roused to life. Thirty to sixty seconds. *There is no way to predict in an individual treatment the exact number of treatments required.*

I have never thought of you on that table, though, until now.

Once, you told me, the doc put some Thorazine in the drip to send you soft and sweet into sleep. A kindness. He knew how you hated this bargain. You told me you wanted to stay there forever.

I sometimes go to the cafeteria for more coffee, a granola bar, something to do. It's still mostly empty so I can sit alone, anywhere. I watch the time, look at the newspaper, return far too early to the waiting room. I never call anyone; I never text updates.

The doctor tells me later: He had a good seizure; I think he's responding. Perhaps another week of treatments. You can see him soon.

After, we drive home in the early spring light, get something to eat: your choice. Sometimes there was a dream, usually a headache, vague fear when you wake. I remark that it's time to take your usual medications. I know you must be hungry so I ask you where you'd like to get some food. A vague shrug. We'll end up in the coffee shop with to-go cups and pastries. I don't ask you how it went: neither one of us have any idea what has happened.

Italicized clinical information about ECT as submitted under oath to County of Ramsey, MN District Court by ███████████████ *, MD, 9/1/2015*

Day 11

Whose gemstone is iced coffee.

Much shuffling, the getting-ready-to;
interview, exam, appointment, ill-

considered or glad, here we sit
on neutral turf, crosswalk, DMZ,

or this happy shelter of over-
stuffed chairs, waiting for

the correct change, no receipt,
long, long rest of the day.

Walgreens: everything plus your meds

You can get a Halloween costume   like ninja or army guy   a santa
hat for the secret santa party   decorations for your tree   you can
buy a new charger for your phone   in case the one that came with
broke   you can get a 12-pack   or whiskey   and cokes to mix with
you can buy a blank journal for your thoughts and journaling   and to
draw   you can buy vitamin b complex   for stress   you can buy a
ton of sharpies   or melatonin   every color or just one color 8-pack
and tape   you can pick up your meds   they send you a text   you
can get mixed nuts in a can or a bag with other stuff   they have pad-
locks   or if you need more shampoo   or half and half   powerades
they have a refrigerated section   also coffee   not already made but
that you can fix   you can get soup   and band-aids   theyre open all
the time   you can get sunglasses   or just the case   sometimes
theres a homeless guy in front

God inside the head of Moses

But he said, "O my Lord, please send someone else."
Exodus 4:13

says get up, get out, you pampered bastard
prince. You weren't born to be
the king. Your swampy birth, pulled fishy
from the reeds, your mother servant
class or worse. You know this, you know this
like you know you're at the center
of something: climate change and politics,

celebrity deaths, revolution. Nights
you pace and write, write and pace,
try to sort it out. One: you're being
groomed for something, the internships,
study abroad, fake command of empire,
labor: stone upon stone upon stone
to heaven. Two: the scepter keeps turning

to a serpent. Repeat: The scepter
keeps turning to a serpent. Three.
You can't contain the curse: slaughter, storm,
contagion, exodus, revolt, judgment
(you're at the center of something). The dream
each night keeps pounding: the roar of hooves,
the wall of water, the boxwoods all on fire.

Results of the Assessments II

Millon Clinical Multiaxial Inventory: True/False

Lately my strength   when i have im afraid   feel like smashing   i
sometimes feel   in recent weeks   im a very   i try to make   my
moods   *some of these are true and some of them are false*   I often feel
i make friends much   i spend my life   lately i have cut   im a very
erratic   lately ive gone   i feel shaky   i feel i deeply   i have tried
to commit suicide   *this one is true and also false*   i have difficulty
controlling   i take great care   my brain just hasnt   lately ive been
sweating   when im alone   ideas often   i have not seen a car in ten
years   *this one is a trick question*   evil voices   i hate to think   i
feel guilty much   even in good times   i sometimes feel   too many
rules   ever since i was a child   i give up trying   sometimes i find
i never feel   people are trying to make me believe i am crazy   *this
one is true and also false*

Day 17

Whose gemstone is constancy:

the slosh and thump of laundry
cycling like a war dance;

the digital blink of the microwave,
green insistence time stands still;

the knife on the block left
from the execution of lunch.

I want my children home.

What I don't say to my husband

You can take him next time. You
can sit there in the crowded
waiting room of the bi-fucking-
polar clinic. You can wait
in the exhaust of his rage
and shame. We are broken, torn,
cleaving to the last and only
primal thread that ties us flesh
to flesh. You can wait as
your heart rate escalates
every quarter hour past
the scheduled appointment, fearful
he will leave, walk out rattling
and mute, leave that loud room, the TV
always chattering about home makeovers
or low-carb pasta or top of the hour.
The din of illness, chorus
of psychosis grinds while each
one is startled to attention:
the patient that fidgets, distracted;
the patient who jumps to attention
when every name is called;
the patient who greets every person
in the room; the patient with no clear
social boundaries, who volunteers
that CBT has worked great for her,
that the day program is great, that they
have art therapy and animal therapy and that
she's lost one hundred pounds and wants
to lose one hundred more and her mother
agrees, will confirm that Dr. E is great,

a savior. You can take your turn
with this week's resident who
emerges with her clipboard.
It goes like this: You breathe in
and unspool the week's report
(not great!). You tell her that we are
doing everything, *everything*
we can and it is killing everything
we ever had that was good
with our son, and though we will
never, never, ever give up hope,
that hope is all we have,
that springs eternal,
that is the thing with feathers,
the tunnel, the light,
the golden fucking dawn alive
with birdsong and buttered scones—
And you can tell her the truth, too,
because you will never ever see
this one again ever: the truth
that we see only bad ends and worse,
that this week was terror-tangled
sheets and nightmares strobing
at the edge of consciousness;
that we are preparing to lose
our son. And you can let me know
later, when you are home, exactly
what she said. If she wrote
anything down at all.

What the record shows

The cell door slammed behind Rubashov.
—Darkness at Noon

Interrogation lights and grim weather;
    the sun when it does
        shine throbs pale
and late above the prison yard
        and the defectors, shuffling
    mules around the millstone.
Cigarettes are in short supply,
        and your tooth aches.
Six and a half steps across
        and back the span
of your black-tiled cell. The barred window
        a blessing; a scrap of paper,
    nub of charcoal appears twice
          a week and you consider
    a new thesis. Citizen:
this is a mistake. You begin to think
        your self a singularity,
          your self a self with unique
purpose and resistance.

In the hall at night, foot drag
        of the damned, and the herald
    of hands drumming against
steel doors, eyes pressed
    against the peepholes, the sentence
ends when the dull thud of History
        punctuates the base of the brain.

Citizen: the record shows
                    oppositional activity, conversation
          with known agitators, deviance
from Party assignment and a brandy
          toast lifted in a firelit study.   Citizen:
here are the letters from
                    your student, here the ticket stub, the flyer,
          the confession.   Citizen:
What say you?

To the ode tapped on a metal pipe
                    with the rim of your spectacles, thin
          rhythm insistent as a bird pecking
at a nerve, we have instructed no reply:
          Comrade, are you there?
                    Friend, what news?

Pareidolia

A type of illusion or misperception involving a vague or obscure stimulus being perceived as something clear and distinct.
—The Skeptic's Dictionary

Holy tortilla with the Virgin's
mild face peering out from
burnt bubble and pock;
fist of sweet roll like the head
of a saint; man
in the moon; white clouds
plumped to the happy body of cow
or sheep or brontosaurus, child's
imagination loosed on his near heaven.
And the lesser, private visages
found daily: cream stirred
into black coffee;
coins arrayed on the countertop
into eyes, nose, streak
of grime a smile; the flare
and spike of knotted wood
like the face of an old man,
a stern aunt.
        Who has not
wandered without companion
along the frayed edge
of the ordinary, or hunched
with that last pang
of faithlessness in the desert,
divined true revelation?

The holy blaze in the rushing stream?
The echoing cave?
The dry brush startled into flame,
its hiss and crackle
the voice of God.

Day 25

Whose gemstone is rain.

Or the threat of rain, something else
I still don't know the answer to

on the horizon and blowing
across the sky. Its stony cape

bulges, and at the hem weak
light like yesterday's news,

the already solved world, what we
thought we saw coming.

III. A bipolar dozen

With the prescribing doctor, work together to review the options for medication. Different types of bipolar disorder may respond better to a particular type. The side effects can vary between medications and it may take time to discover the best medicine.
—National Alliance on Mental Illness

Abilify

He's tried all forms—
10 mg oral, 300 mg injectable,
400, an inconceivable
number over 1000, straight shot
into the muscle—a vaccine
against noncompliance.
The new doctor believes
in this one; he says
it acts like
a kind of neuro-
pump, adjacent, enabling
rage.

Ativan

Mom, I think
this is working he says
at the first hospital. He
peers up from
the static and thunder
of five days awake,
astonished.

Celexa

Hell no he wouldn't take
it again. He knew
it wasn't right, felt it buzzing
in his veins like a trapped
fly. Wouldn't take a pill
that sounded like the name
of a goddamn luxury sedan,
smooth over winding
mountain roads, silent
into an inferno of fall colors,
flaming in a distant state.

Depakote

Might as well be
called dead-a-kote—
a dumb blunt of
a drug dosed
by the 500 mg
slug. Thuggish,
old-school knockout.

Geodon

Another atypical. It set
his foot twitching,
then tap-tapping, rapid
at dinner on the back deck,
tremors
across the surface
of our filled glasses.

Lithium

Created at the Universe's
brilliant birth, stardust
salted over the fires
in his brain to bring blessed
equilibrium—
it silted
into his soul like lead,
deadening,
then aflame anew.

Luvox

This is the one that started
it all, that he asked for that
first summer, that he thought
would help with what he thought
was wrong, and that was wrong
with lots of people he knew who
were taking a pill. This is the one
that didn't do what it was
promised, that wasn't the slow
lifting of the fog, the tuning of static
into song. This is the one
that unhoused the demons,
should have told us something,
but we never would have
believed it.

Propranolol

Even ordinary people
(i.e., not diagnosed)
can take this as a PRN:
the "stage fright drug."
I'm still trying to
pronounce it correctly.
I imagine trying to
say the name
of it onstage, before
a thousand, thousand faces,
none of them listening.

Remeron

Side effects can include nightmares,
worse than the ones he's living.
It's supposed to help
with sleep, that magical cave
of the good night's rest, a serious
dose of REM, hence the name.
But it didn't work. No
sleeping, no nightmares.

Risperdal

I wasn't sure how to pronounce
it, where the accent fell. I kept
spelling it wrong. I wasn't
stupid. We just couldn't
hear what the doctor
was saying.

Seroquel

He only took one dose.
It caused that scary thing
where the muscles
constrict, shortness of breath.
I visited him in the day room
at the third hospital, watched him
clutch his throat, puffing out
quick exhalations. I told the
nurse, who paled. Did not
request another dose.

Trazodone

Heavy lifting, that
Trazodone, a mighty
bulldozer of a med shoving
up the damp sod
of sleep. Pill-wise
it dosed high: 50, 100 mg.
It didn't work.

Vistaril

It sounded like
the name of a travel
company, a motor coach line,
some way to get somewhere
clear, where the view
is fine.

Zyprexa

He stayed on this one
a long time—relatively
speaking—10 mg, then
15 mg, then at 20
it was lights out, in a stupor
on the couch. I'd find
him sometimes like that
on dark afternoons.

IV. Whose gemstone is rain

What you are feeling is grief

*Don't ever tell anybody anything. If you
do, you'll start missing everybody.*
—Holden Caulfield

Holden, you were never well.
The manic scene of roommate
trouble, the antics and the prattle,
the failed exams, the hustle out
through empty halls, the shrieked
farewell to old Pencey Prep, the train
to the city and all *that madman stuff*
that happened there—

you never slept.

You contrive to meet a friend, revive
a romance, spend all your money
on tickets, drinks. You never eat.
You see salvation in every face
and stepping from the curb
dissociate. The phoniness
is not a joke. There's nothing
there. The carousel goes around
and rain comes down. Someone
must have found you crying
there. And now the quiet place
where you rest is locked,
white-coated, clean. There is
a schedule, plan for discharge,
release. Telling your story
is part of the healing, they
will say. I hope they are kind.

Everyone has been so

theres a guy at our church   could you get him involved   service could
be an option or volunteer   maybe a dog   he needs to be outside   do
you think he would like   what about volunteer   have you talked to
anyone at habitat   I have a friend whose son   maybe he could find
they usually need people   theres habitat too   our daughters friend
has a group   he needs to find meaningful   what about fixing up the
basement into   our nephew had a great experience with   one of our
neighbors works for habitat   maybe I could connect you with   Ive
heard that winter can be bad for   have you called   this was a long
time ago but my stepbrother had a lot of luck with   this guy at work
mentioned habitat   I saw an article about support animals   maybe a
lawyer or someone who   structure is so   have you tried the website
for habitat   my sons roommate did work one summer for   have you
tried   theres habitat   maybe you could contact   habitat   is there
anyone   habitat   *yes*   *we appreciate you all*

Near you, not touching

What shall Cordelia speak? Love, and be silent.
—Act 1, scene 1, *King Lear*

She wants no thing this day
                    or ever: not money
          for gas, not breakfast nor
her laundry folded,
                    not the litany
of my day, my
          purchases and tasks. She wants
no comments
          on the weather, the grocery list,
                    the war in France.
                              She haunts the palace, imperious,
pacing through the galleries, the tower
          walk; opening cabinets or idly
clicking at her screen. Our shadows
          sometimes pass near enough to darken
                    a slant of late day light. She is mass
          enough for whisper, hand's glance
to shoulder, voice enough
          for greeting, ritual thanks.
At night she slips past
                    my embrace, closes her door and doesn't
hear me howl, the keening
          grief of love on its knees.

Waiting for the Resurrection

I.

It is Holy Week, and I am fracture critical, in
                        colony collapse, my hive mind
            disordered, synchronous hum
                        like a death buzz
                                    against smudged
windows.   There is pain in my leg, always

                        the taste of salt
        in my throat. I do not sleep,
                    I mostly eat
standing up.   I despair; I see

        only bad ends and worse.   No
                        narratives of normalcy apply, no
                        memes of errand and accomplishment, no
to-do lists, bucket lists, checklists
                    of dinners we've dreamed
        of having. This is not just the trouble
                    with traffic and don't we all wish.
I despair

        of morning, despair of evening, the blotchy night.
                    There is only a hermit in a rocky cave, seaside
and delusional,
        his vision settling like fog over rocks, like blood
                    into water, like chalk clapped from
                                cracked palms.
I am alone and blown,
                        it is getting dark,
                and I have started to pray.

II.

When a morning starts silver-polishing
busy, where is there to go when
already eggs and toast on the deck

for breakfast and a second pot
of coffee and the whole *New York Times*
read and refolded by nine, where then?

What busyness will keep us further
from despair? How will we greet
the noon already exhausted

with errand and repair? How will we
stagger through the afternoon when
it really will be hot, proceed to evening

still standing after this white-knuckled
slide of to-do and checked-off, every plant
that needs watering, every sheet that needs

laundering? We will need
more ice and we will need
a drink and we will need

darkness as soon as it can get here.

III.

Anxious that the meat is too done   is not done that the casserole will
not set   that the pan will not deglaze without the right wine   Anx-
ious bringing each hot dish to the sideboard   Anxious when the water
in the silver pitcher runs out   Anxious for the prayer   for the serving
the first fork lifted too soon and then rested   Anxious for the bread to
be passed   the butter at the wrong end of the table   Anxious that one
will eat quickly and want to leave   another too slowly and I'll have to
stay   that I won't be able to stay   Anxious as one plate is cleaned and
another is set coffee cake berries whipped topping   the froth of
it all   like thunderclouds gathering on the hill

It's just been a difficult week

Depression and Bipolar Support Alliance, weekly meeting for supporters

We have a lot of new faces tonight so just a few ground rules   Im here for my daughter who suffers from depression and also myself maybe we should split into two groups   its been a long journey for my brother   this is our first night   please share your name if youre comfortable   our son has been diagnosed   my wife has had a relapse   Im sorry I should say my name   its just been a difficult week and its been a while since weve come   does anyone have a rager   have you tried the shot form you dont have to worry   I think we know what the triggers are   we also have some handouts and there will be   I cant get her to talk to someone so thats why I came tonight   he balls his fists and goes to his room but we can hear I was hoping   my wifes psychiatrist has her on a lot of different meds is he able to communicate   my husband has had a lot of luck with dbt which is different from cbt   so its hard to tell   if you can find a doc-tor who will listen   so its hard to know   this is my first night   we have an affirmation   has she been cutting herself again   Im sorry we have one more person to speak and then the affirmation   we cant tell because the boyfriend   I know some of you need to   what is the shot form   but lets stand and if you want to hold hands   my daughter just texted   thats fine or just remain silent   my daughter just texted   please I know some of you need   my daughter just tex-ted I need   and also a dollar for the coffee

Blood sport sabbath

I.

The hounds are wild.

One coon treed, its mate burrowed
in the brush pile and screaming.
They claw through dead branches,
collapsed wire fencing, briars, old lumber,
howl their bloodsong, insensible
to the litany of their sired names, the command
to *Leave it!* They find
purchase in a ringed tail,
drag the creature to the surface, tear
into meat and fur until the crack
of the huntsman's pistol quiets all
but the wind breaking in the winter trees.

The dogs stand down, obedient
under the huntsman's strange patter,
and scatter
snuffle the damp ground for new quarry,
the scent rising
in the warm afternoon. We follow in a ragged line, uneasy
about the weather. We know
that the day should be colder, mercy more certain,

that there is no getting right with this god.

II.

Winter-thinned and brittle,
the native grasses rise
shoulder high, snap
under our tread, our
descent into the brush
following the pack.
We urge the hounds
toward scent, wait
for their primitive
blood to flare
with the chase. Straining
at the edge of wild when
the horn sounds, they
swarm from the dark
hollow, rush
the quarry over hills.
Hunched into
the morning sun,
we startle
at the white flash
of the hare
hard upon us.

III.

We are not the hounds,
and we are not the quarry,
and we are not the One In Charge.
We are not the quail
flushed from a thicket of briars,
nor the vultures overhead,
their black wings carving
circles against lush blue,
nor the three, white-tailed deer
bounding away from the path.
We are not the thorn,
nor the redbud piercing into bloom,
not the improbable geometry
of the falling rock wall,
not the geese in formation.
We are not the sound of the horn,
not the crack of the whip.
We are not the sighting,
not the scent,
not the kill.

We were talking about our fathers' guns

We were talking about guns   at the luncheon after the funeral   and my friend had discovered   his dead dads gun   in the dresser just one bullet   and a hole   where once   and we all laughed about this   he had accidentally discharged the weapon   trying   to unload it   probably killed   all the socks in the drawer   haha   and then another shared about how her dad   one time   insisting this things not loaded   shot a hole in the kitchen door   his wifes arms crossed I told you so   and the holes still there to this day   and so I turn to my dad and say so   do we even know where all your guns are   and we laughed   haha   because we know theyre all under the bed   the long guns anyway   under the bed in the master bedroom where nobody sleeps anymore except me when I visit   but what about the pistols I ask   how many pistols did we find anyway when we cleaned out grandpas house   boxes of ledgers and bottles of that whiskey with his name on it and the things from his bank office   and he said   quieter   several   dad gave me his pistols   sometime after mother died and he told me   here   I dont need to have these around   I dont know   my dad said looking at his beer   depressed maybe   but he didnt want to have them around   I remembered then how I found that one   a long time later   still unpacking boxes   it was small maybe what I thought a derringer was   but I dont really know what a derringer is really   at the bottom of a box   I pulled it out and asked my dad   whats this   probably a gun he said then   it was wrapped in dark leather   soft as an old womans skin   its gray heft warm   as if hed just been holding it

Security: A Q & A

*What was your favorite part-time job? What do you
do to relax? What was the first musical
instrument you learned to play?*
                              Everybody learned recorder in fourth grade.
What is the first name of one of your bridesmaids?
                              That's getting a little personal, I think
                                        and oddly specific. I had four bridesmaids—
                              how do I choose? I have some security

questions myself, like: Am I in danger
          here and how fast is the storm coming and
do we need to shelter in place? And what of
                    the contagion and if I show symptoms:
Is it too late? What of locks and bolts and shutters and bars?

Security Question #1: Have you established a successor?
Security Question #2: Are there enough PFDs on board for every passenger?
Security Question #3: Dried and canned is best for the long haul.
                              That's not really a question. And I still
                    have a lot of questions.
Answer please: What was the name of your first pet?
                    Question: What are matches, potable water, reflection
                                        blankets, tinned peaches.
Answer please: What is the name of the city where your parents met?
                    They weren't always happy, though it looked
                              that way. And then the marriage dissolved.
                    We were all okay in the end.

Answer please: What was the make of your first car?
                    What if I forget the code?

The alarm will go off at the server and security will come.
            Will they have guns?
Will you? After three attempts you will be locked out.
            That sounds bad. What if
                        I can't remember?

Why didn't you write it down?

Coleridge at his study

A grief without a pang, void, dark, and drear,
A stifled, drowsy, unimpassioned grief,
Which finds no natural outlet, no relief,
In word, or sigh, or tear—
—"Dejection: An Ode"

sighs 'O.' Sleepless still at midnight,
a storm surges outside
his study. He can see,
but cannot feel,
act but cannot ache.
Stanza by stanza he sings
his dissolution. Sorry, sorry
says the wind, and moans
the Mad Lutanist his despair,
striking imagined strings,
stretched across an imagined
hollow box. His spirit numbs
to clap of thunder, crack of lightning—
O something to prick this shell,
this façade silent at the carapace
of the very abyss! O dulled senses!
O dulled spirit!

The rain slashes at the sill,
and still he scribbles, blots.
He recalls incandescent stars
sifting through a sieve of clouds,
drifting like skiffs on a celestial sea.
He documents their excellence,
but cannot feel the soul-sent
Joy, *O Lady!* How well he

knows his own psychosis:
the devils and dark dreams,
the vipers coiling in his mind.
The Mad Lutanist screams
a devil's tune, the wind skelps
a barren mountain. Things get
tangled here and the metaphor
is lost. A vision fills the room:
a tide of men groaning
from the cold and trampled
in an anxious rush; a shuddering
silence; and almost solid now,
a child lost on the moor, keening
for her mother. And still the wind
howls on—

The vision dims, but for
a benediction for slumber
half-delivered to *O Lady!*
as if saying it might
save him. It will not.
He will not sleep for days.

What did or didn't happen later

"Quentin? Is he sick, Mr MacKenzie?"

Clear high tinkle of the store bell   behind you the girl   slick braids
and nickel in her dirty fist   the malformed knot of cake from the clerk
she reminds you of someone   follows you out and sticks   watching
and not talking   you ask and ask   later you take her down to the
little row houses   a few words to get her home   no one will take her
the paper on the wrapped loaf fraying like a hem   she'll get in trouble
she reminds you of someone   later the brother   rage and accusations
the law and time   never on the side of honor   later you can't stop
laughing   the ridiculous car and the hamper of wine   you see her
in the lane at the gate and wave   what happened or didn't   scrap
of newspaper against the wall   she reminds you of someone   the
timepiece in your pocket   the quarter hour and the three-quarters
clanging in the square   the six pound flat-irons that are heavy enough
later you remember   so beautiful there in the water   hair splayed on
the sand   the smell of rain   honeysuckle   and the sky   so   low

Pray for Rain

Beautiful girl,
like a tall drink of water,
let me tell you

of such a singing:
of dry furrows, patch
of thistle, what subsists

in hardship and root,

how ruinous love, with
its excuses of silence
and thunder falls.

I sent a son out into
the world,
graceful and steady as rain.

Notes

The opening epigraph and also to "What you are feeling is grief" are from *The Catcher in the Rye* by J.D. Salinger.

"Reading a biography of Robert Lowell I think": The epigraph is from a letter to Ezra Pound from Robert Lowell as recounted in *Robert Lowell: Setting the River on Fire* by Kay Redfield Jamison.

"Dear F. Scott": The epigraph is from a letter to Malcom Cowley from F. Scott Fitzgerald as recounted in *Zelda: A Biography* by Nancy Milford.

"What the record shows": The epigraph is the first line from Arthur Koestler's novel *Darkness at Noon.*

The epigraph for Section III is from nami.org, "Bipolar Disorder: treatment"

"Coleridge at his study": The epigraph is from Samuel Taylor Coleridge's poem "Dejection: An Ode."

"What did or didn't happen later": The epigraph is from *The Sound and the Fury* by William Faulkner.

Biographical Note

Lynnell Edwards is a poet, writer, teacher, and author of six collections of poetry, most recently *This Great Green Valley* (Broadstone Books, 2020). She serves as Associate Programs Director for the Sena Jeter Naslund-Karen Mann Graduate School of Writing at Spalding University, where she is faculty in poetry and also book reviews editor for *Good River Review*. She lives in Louisville, Kentucky.

Printed in the USA
CPSIA information can be obtained
at www.ICGtesting.com
JSHW021048280224
58160JS00002B/2